TABLE OF CONTENTS

Acknowledgements...................................v

Preface...vii

How To Use This Book............................ix

Reference Guide.................................xi

Objections and Responses........................1

THE YELLOW PAGES HANDBOOK

OF

OBJECTIONS
and
RESPONSES

---

by
Jeffrey Price

Idlewood Publishing, Pacific Palisades, California

THE YELLOW PAGES HANDBOOK
OF
Objections
and
Responses

by
Jeffrey Price

Published by: Idlewood Publishing
Pacific Palisades, California

Copyright ©1988 by Jeffrey Price
Printed in the United States of America

ISBN 0-945909-00-4

ACKNOWLEDGEMENTS

Thanks to Linda Rodgers for her suggestions and editorial assistance.

Thanks to Joan Boswell and R. H. Regart for their responses to my daily barrage of questions when I first began selling yellow pages advertising.

PREFACE

Following is the most complete list of objections that yellow pages salespeople commonly encounter, along with several proven responses to each one.

The list was prepared by Jeffrey Price, a former sales trainer, sales manager and top yellow pages salesman for both the Telephone and Independent Directory Companies. During his career, Mr. Price was recognized as a master at overcoming sales objections.

This handbook should be studied, reviewed and kept handy by any yellow pages salesperson who wants to sharpen his skills and increase sales. New or inexperienced salespeople will benefit from this handbook because they often lack or forget information needed to effectively respond to objections. Seasoned salespeople will benefit from it because it offers them fresh approaches to replace stale ones.

An indispensible tool, this handbook is a vital first step to increased productivity for yellow pages salespeople everywhere.

W.F. Wagner
Author of
Advertising in the Yellow Pages

HOW TO USE THIS BOOK

On the following page you will find a quick reference guide. For your convenience, it is broken down into the three categories that usually give rise to sales objections—cost, usage and value.

Locate the category you need. You will be referred by page number to the objection and possible responses. If you can't find the objection you're looking for, check the other categories.

This book is designed for use at any time. Carry it with you and use it, if possible, on sales calls. Refer to it *after* a sales call if you feel you haven't adequately responded to a customer's objection. Next time that objection arises, you'll be ready. Study it at your leisure so you become expert at handling objections.

Don't try to memorize the responses. Simply understand the basic theme of a response. Then play it back to your customers in your own words.

The best way to become proficient at handling objections is to repeatedly test yourself. Pose an objection and respond out loud until you can say it comfortably and convincingly.

REFERENCE GUIDE

Cost

Business Is Terrible...1

We're Cutting Expenses....................................3

My Budget Is Committed.................................4

I Can't Afford It..5

Another Directory? I'm
    Spending Too Much On
    My Yellow Pages As It Is.............................6

It Costs Too Much...8

The Rates Are Too High....................................9

If Your Rates Have Gone Up,
    Cancel My Ad..11

Advertising In More Than One
    Directory Is A Duplication........................12

I'd Have To Advertise At Too
    Many Headings...13

My Ad In The Other Directory
    Works Just Fine..15

I've Already Signed Up With
    The Phone Company...................................16

Everyone In This Classification
    Has Agreed Not To Advertise.....................17

Usage

I Already Tried Yellow Pages
   Advertising With No Results......................18

I Wish There Were Just
   One Directory...21

No One Would Look For Me
   In The Yellow Pages...................................22

If People Want Me, They Know
   How To Find Me...23

I Never Use The Yellow Pages 25

I Used A Test Number And
   Got No Results...27

You're Not The Phone Company......................28

I Didn't Get That Book Delivered
   To My House...29

I Don't Think People Use
   Your Book...31

People Throw Away Your Book.......................32

I've Talked To My Friends And
   Neighbors, And They Don't Use
   Your Book. I'm Not Renewing My Ad.........34

How Do I Know You'll Deliver
   Your Books?..36

People Only Use The Book With
   The White Pages...37

Value

Just Leave It Like It Is.....................................39

I've Gone Over This Before And I'm
    Just Not Interested 41

All My Business Comes By
    Word-Of-Mouth...43

I've Decided To Cancel All
    My Advertising..44

I'll Just Wait Until Next Year.......................... 45

Let Me Think It Over...................................... 47

I Don't Need A Larger Ad.............................. 48

I Only Want A Bold Listing............................. 50

I'm Not Interested...51

Call Me When The Book Is Closing................. 53

There Are Just Too Many Directories..............55

I Use Other Forms Of Advertising...................57

Everybody Knows Me......................................60

My Competition Has Only A Listing.................63

I Have More Business Than
    I Can Handle...65

Yellow Pages Isn't For My Kind
    Of Business... 66

My Ad Doesn't Pull Like It Used To.................67

Let Me Talk To My Partner.............................69

I Do No Local Business...................................70

My Business Is Seasonal.................................71

We Have Our Own Sales Force.......................72

Can You Guarantee The
    Position I Want?...74

My Business Is Too Small..............................76

I'm Selling My Business................................77

There Are Already Too Many Ads
    At My Heading...78

Mine Is A Cash And
    Carry Business..79

I've Had A Lot Of Problems
    With Your Company....................................80

I'm Moving..81

I Never Advertise...83

I'd Only Get Nuisance Calls...........................84

My Location Brings In All
    My Business..86

I Have No Competition...................................88

I Can't Get Good Help...................................89

Will You Guarantee It Works?.........................89

People Don't Look At Big Ads.........................90

As A Professional, I Have
    An Ethical Problem About
    Advertising In The Yellow Pages.................92

The Big Boys In My Line Don't Advertise
   In The Yellow Pages.....................................93

Yellow Pages Advertising Would
   Lock Me In For Too Long
   A Period Of Time..95

I Deal Only With a Few Firms...........................97

I'll Only Deal With
   Last Year's Salesperson..............................98

I Don't Want To Be Associated With
   The Riff-Raff At My Heading.....................101

I Had A Bad Experience With An
   Independent Directory Company..............102

There Aren't Many Ads
   At My Classification.................................103

Let Me See How Your Book
   Does This Year...104

1. BUSINESS IS TERRIBLE.

A. If that's the case, you've got to look at your situation and realize whatever you're doing isn't working out well. You must be willing to make some changes.

Favorable turns in the general economy or in your particular industry may take too long to occur. There's no reason why you must weather slow periods which so drastically affect your cash flow.

Yellow pages advertising is designed in an extremely cost-effective way to attract new customers to your business. It's this kind of change you need to make which will increase sales for you.

B. I understand how you feel. A sense of fear sets in when business is slow, and you want to reduce costs. A lot of business owners feel the same as you under those conditions.

Still, it's important to remember that all businesses are built on sales. When business is off, you need to make even more sales and get more customers.

Did you know that 9 out of 10 people use the yellow pages as a buyers guide? Doesn't it make good sense to be advertising to people you've never done business with before who are ready to buy exactly what you sell?

This is how your new customer base grows. Of course, what follows the growth of new customers is an increase in your word-of-mouth business as well.

2. WE'RE CUTTING EXPENSES.

A. When I hear a business owner say this, it means one thing and one thing only: Not enough sales are being generated for that particular business.

All businesses need to make sales to survive and grow. When business has fallen off, it is even more important to focus on increasing sales. To reduce a business's visibility with its potential customers is not the last thing that should be done. Rather, it should never be done!

The best way to increase your business is to increase the number of your customers. That is exactly what I do for many businesses in the area. I can do it for your business as well, through yellow pages advertising.

B. That is an excellent business policy as long as you're cutting non-productive expenses and not productive expenses. Yellow pages advertising is a productive expense be-

3

cause it brings the buyer to the seller at that special moment— when the buyer is ready to make a purchase. It not only pays for itself, it helps pay other costs which cannot be cut.

3. MY BUDGET IS COMMITTED.

A. A very successful businessman once told me that "It's good sense to budget your business, but it's better sense to be flexible." I think what he was referring to was being in a position to seize opportunities when they arise.

If I asked you to take a five dollar bill out of your pocket and hand it over to me on the condition that I would exchange it for a ten dollar bill, you would do it, wouldn't you? You'd probably make that kind of transaction all day, am I right? What would you do if that original five dollar bill weren't in your budget? You'd change your budget, wouldn't you? That's what I'm asking you to do now with regard to your yellow pages advertising. Change your budget so you can seize a very profitable opportunity.

B. Budgets are important, yet they need to be flexible. If you spent all the money you allocated for truck repairs and your truck broke down, you wouldn't let the truck stand idle until your next fiscal budget came around, would you? Of course not, because the truck helps you make money. Advertising is no different. I've come here today to show you how yellow pages advertising can help you make money.

4. I CAN'T AFFORD IT.

A. Let me ask you a question. How can you not afford to make money? Did you ever ask yourself why so many businesses would advertise in the yellow pages if it weren't a money making venture?

B. Advertising in the yellow pages isn't something that costs, it pays. It's my job to be familiar with the various rates charged for advertising one's business. I know yellow pages' rates happen to be nearly the lowest of all media available to you. When you tell me you can't afford yellow pages advertising, that tells me you need more customers. Is that a correct assessment of your current business situation? Well, that is precisely what advertising in the yellow pages does for millions of businesses like yours. It directs people who are ready to buy to your telephone and to your front door.

5. ANOTHER DIRECTORY? I'M SPENDING TOO MUCH ON MY YELLOW PAGES AS IT IS.

A. Let me ask you, do you feel your yellow pages ads are working? If you feel they are, then you're not spending too much. As a matter of fact, you're not spending at all—you're *making* a profit. Even though you may feel rates are high, the ads are still bringing in more dollars than you pay for your ads every month. Our advertisers are making money, too, because not everyone uses the same directory. Many people use both. There's no reason why you can't profit by being in both directories as well.

If, on the other hand, your ads are bringing in business, but not enough to cover your current advertising rates, let me show you how you can get the same or greater coverage and reduce your cost considerably.

B. You may be experiencing what a lot of other businesses in your situation are. Your ads aren't bringing in as many dollars as you'd like. Apparently, you're investing all your money in one or maybe two directories. However, when one of our many users looks in our directory, you don't get any business. Other businesses have found a profitable solution to be this. They spend those same dollars but spread them equally among the directories in their area. That way their yellow pages dollar is working for them, no matter *which* directory is used.

6. IT COSTS TOO MUCH.

A. Isn't cost a relative term? A house costs a lot of money, yet it provides you with daily shelter, comfort and pleasure. If real estate values rise significantly from the date of purchase, it is certainly a worthwhile investment and doesn't cost too much.

When considering any kind of advertising, you want to look at cost—yet you also need to focus on the return. Will I make money? Will this advertising be cost effective for my business? If you want the answer to those questions, look at the large number of businesses that renew and increase their yellow pages advertising each year.

B. Let me ask you something. Which ad do you think costs more? This display ad that measures 5"x 5" or this bold listing? I'm not kidding when I tell you the bold listing costs considerably more. The number of customers and the amount of business generated from that bold listing is significantly less than the volume of business the large display ad attracts. Even though the monthly rate for the display ad is much more than that of the bold listing, the net profit is far greater for the display ad. Isn't it the net profit or return and not the cost that you should be concerned with?

7. THE RATES ARE TOO HIGH.

A. That's really only true if your return doesn't meet or exceed your investment. If you were to travel to any town or city in this country, there would be a yellow pages directory filled with advertisers of businesses just like yours.

If business owners weren't finding yellow pages advertising profitable, the number of advertisers in these directories would greatly diminish. The fact of the matter is however, that the yellow pages industry has been growing faster than any other advertising media because businesses are investing more money today in yellow pages advertising than ever before.

B. At the stage we're at now, I can understand your feeling that yellow pages advertising rates are too high. All you're focused on are 12 monthly payments. Let's look at the end result. After all, you don't pass judgment on your entire fiscal year when you're in your second quarter.

What you'll discover is what so many other business owners already know. Yellow pages rates aren't too high because the investment generates an impressive return.

8. IF YOUR RATES HAVE GONE UP, CANCEL MY AD.

A. I understand how you feel, no one wants to pay more for something. However, that shouldn't be the only deciding factor in whether to keep your ads in the directory. It makes sense to advertise as long as it's profitable. Even though your advertising rates may have gone up, that does not mean your ads won't bring in more business than ever before.

B. Even though our rates have gone up from last year, they still represent a tremendous value for your advertising dollar. Compare our rates to other print media, like radio, magazines or television. You'll see that we're not only the least expensive per household, but that we *remain* in the household. Remember, we guarantee our rates for one year while other advertising media can (and often do) raise their rates several times a year.

9. ADVERTISING IN MORE THAN ONE DIRECTORY IS A DUPLICATION.

A. While it is true your ad in our directory would be reaching basically the same people as in the other directory, it's really not a duplication. Some people will refer to our competitor's directory while others will refer only to ours. Many people will often use both directories, placing one in the kitchen and the other in the den or office. By representing yourself in both books, you are ensuring you'll be seen, no matter which book is used.

B. The yellow pages is no different from T.V., radio, and newspapers. It's quite common for companies to advertise on more than one network, be heard on more than one radio station and be represented in rival newspapers. This is because the general public has varied habits and references. When it comes to usage, the yellow pages is no different from other advertising media. There is no evidence that only one directory is being used anymore than only one T.V. channel is being watched.

10. I'D HAVE TO ADVERTISE AT TOO MANY HEADINGS.

A. You've just stated the best reason for having a developed program in the yellow pages. When a customer comes in and makes a purchase, you make a profit, don't you? Well, the yellow pages is really nothing more than a vehicle to bring in customers. The more headings you advertise under, the more customers you're likely to get.

B. Correct me if I'm wrong, but it seems that your real concern is about the cost of advertising under a lot of headings. People advertise in the yellow pages year after year for one reason: *it's profitable.* You're fortunate that you're not in a one-classification business. This way, you can promote each phase of your business, bringing in many new customers and maximizing your results.

C. The headings that represent your business in the yellow pages are there because businesses, like yours, have discovered that's where potential customers look for them.

D. Picture a large department store. It has several entrances where most of the people enter the store. It also has a number of other entrances for the convenience of the rest of the shoppers. These doors are similar to headings in a directory. You can represent yourself with large ads under your most important classifications and place smaller ads under other related classifications.

E. That shouldn't be a reason for you not to represent yourself in the directory. If you're able to place advertising in 5 or 10 classifications that pertain to your business,

I recommend it because it will be profitable. If you only want to represent yourself under one heading, then I recommend that as well. Even though your results will reflect a smaller profit, it still justifies the investment.

11. MY AD IN THE OTHER DIRECTORY WORKS JUST FINE.

A. Great! Then you've found an advertising medium that works well for you. If you're making money from the yellow pages, why limit yourself to just one directory?

B. When you're watching television, you don't see Coke or Pepsi advertised on only one network, do you? Of course not. They've found it profitable to advertise on all the networks because not everyone watches one channel. The yellow pages is no different. Some people use the directory I represent, others use the one you advertise in, and many use both directories.

12. I'VE ALREADY SIGNED UP WITH THE PHONE COMPANY.

A. Well, if you've signed up with the phone company, that means you must be a believer in yellow pages advertising, is that right? So what I need to do is to prove our product is being used, correct?

Because you own a business you know that not all yellow pages directories are published by the phone company. Your customer, however, does not get solicited by sales representatives and is often unaware of the different publishers. As a matter of fact, they frequently assume that all yellow pages are published by their phone company. When they pick up a yellow pages directory they believe it's a phone company product, especially since the phone company prints and distributes so many different books today.

B. That's fine, I'm sure you'll get good results when someone picks up that directory and sees your ad. What kind of results do you think you'll get when someone picks up our directory and only sees your competitor's ad?

13. EVERYONE AT THIS CLASSIFICATION HAS AGREED NOT TO ADVERTISE.

A. It sounds as though you feel advertising in the yellow pages is an expense and that in the end it will cost you money. That is just not true. As a matter of fact, millions of businesses decide every year to invest their advertising dollars in the yellow pages because it will make them money. Those business owners who are advertising for the first time feel it's a good investment, those who have advertised before know it's one.

B. On a few rare occasions, I've seen that attempted. Do you know what always happened? A couple of business owners got scared others would end up advertising and they'd be left out, and they placed ads at the last minute. You may have gotten a sound agreement from all your competitors, but there's always the possibility of someone new opening up in your area (a likely candidate for advertising) or someone from outside your area advertising to attract your customers.

It's very difficult to coordinate a boycott. And you're doing it for all the wrong reasons. Why would you want to hide from the people who are in need of your product or service, particularly when they keep you in business?

14. I ALREADY TRIED YELLOW PAGES ADVERTISING WITH NO RESULTS.

A. Which sourcing method did you use to determine you got no results? Actually, other business owners have felt the same as you feel because of impressions or perceptions of poor results. Yet they agreed that

that's all they were— impressions, not facts.

It's very difficult for many business owners to accurately source every telephone call or every customer who comes through the front door. Customers really have no reason to say they've arrived via your yellow pages ad.

In all fairness to you and your business, you must accurately determine whether your ad was profitable. This means sourcing every customer during the course of the entire year.

If that's too difficult for you because you're busy with things like payroll, inventory or sales, let me show you the results of other business owners who insisted on attaining such information.

You know, the mere presence of the same advertisers in your classification should tell you that advertising in the yellow pages can be very profitable for your business.

B. Mr. Phillips, your business is no different than the many others that advertise in the yellow pages each year. Chances are you got good results from your ad but just don't know it. Let me explain why.

There are basically two ways to determine whether someone is responding to your yellow pages ad. Either your customer volunteers that information, or you and your employees ask for the information.

Most word-of-mouth recommendations go unmentioned so it's unlikely for customers to explain how they found you. Many business owners tell us that they and their employees are either reluctant or too busy to ask every caller (telephone or walk-in) that question.

Your customers have found you in many ways— passing by, a recommendation, or through the yellow pages. But without asking, you'll never know this important information.

Let me show you a number of ways to determine how your ad is working.

15. I WISH THERE WERE JUST ONE DIRECTORY.

A. You probably also wish there were just one business like yours in town. Unfortunately that's not how things are. In a free enterprise system people have a choice of doing business with you or your competition and you have that same choice in yellow pages advertising. I'm here today to tell you about the customers you'll attract by advertising in this directory.

B. I agree that if there were just one yellow pages directory, you'd be certain which directory was being used. However, that kind of a situation doesn't mean it would be any more cost effective for you. Only one yellow pages publisher in your area would constitute a monopoly. They could charge whatever they wanted to for representation in the book. More than one directory means competition, and that generally keeps prices in line. By advertising in two directories, you might be spending fewer dollars than if there were just one book in town.

16. NO ONE WOULD LOOK FOR ME IN THE YELLOW PAGES.

A. Let me ask you, if someone were looking for you in the yellow pages, and you weren't there, how would you know they were looking for you?

B. During the course of a year, do you do business with people who have just moved into the area, have an emergency, are dissatisfied with another company, seldom purchase particular products or services you offer, or who have compared your prices with others? Then people have been looking for you in the directory because I've just described the types of buyers who refer to the yellow pages every day.

C. They may not be looking for you in particular, but they're looking for someone who offers the same goods and services you carry. You're entitled to that business as much as your competitors are.

D. You mean no one *finds* you in the yellow pages. With the type of listing you have compared to the advertising your competitors have, it's no surprise your customers don't come to you through the yellow pages. Your competition has been making it easy to do business with them by providing all the information that triggers people to call.

17. IF PEOPLE WANT ME, THEY KNOW HOW TO FIND ME.

A. There are many different types of customers, and there are many different ways of soliciting them. Some of the people you do business with come here by way of word-of-mouth. Some are passersby, and others are influenced by your advertising. There is still another market out there, larger than you may ever imagined, that you have left untapped. That market consists of people who are ready to buy exactly what you're selling but don't know who carries it. They turn to a convenient directory— the yellow pages. It's a book they've been familiar with all their lives that gives them the information they're looking for.

B. I wouldn't surprise you by making the statement that we live in a transient society, would I? In many areas of the country, 20% of the population has an address change each year. A major user of the yellow pages is the person who has recently moved to an area because everything is new and unfamiliar to them. These newcomers typically don't know people to ask for recommendations. Whether they'll be in the area for one year or the next twenty, don't you want their business?

C. They may *want* you, but perhaps they don't *know* you. In other words, they want your product or service yet they've never done business with you before. These buyers are looking for you. So why hide? Make yourself visible with a large ad in a directory they turn to every day when they don't know where to get what they need.

D. What about the people doing business with your competition for the first time? They might have done business with you if they had known about you. I can show you how to get your fair share of that business.

18. I NEVER USE THE YELLOW PAGES.

A. That may be so but did you know that 9 out of 10 adults do use the yellow pages? What's important to a business owner like you is that these people only use the directory when they're ready to buy.

B. A lot of business owners don't use the yellow pages because they've been doing business with the same suppliers for years and have their names and phone numbers on their rolodex, on business cards or even memorized. Yet your customer is a consumer, not someone running a business. The yellow pages, to them, is not some new or novel idea. They have been using it as a buyers information guide for more than 100 years.

C. I think you'll agree that in a capitalistic society like ours, people's tastes and habits are diverse. Look at all the different types of cars, stereo equipment, or telephones manufactured today. Look at the different ways people get their exercise— bicycling, jogging, walking, tennis. Even though you don't use the yellow pages, I can prove to you that others do. As a matter of fact, the yellow pages are used by 9 out of 10 adults.

19. I USED A TEST NUMBER AND GOT NO RESULTS.

A. Do you mind if I take a look at your telephone log or tally sheet? If you haven't set up a log or tally sheet, instructed every employee to record all incoming calls (regardless of which line they come in on) and ensured this procedure is being followed every day you're open for business, I'm afraid your results aren't valid. I'm sure you'll want to keep the advertising if it's profitable for your business. The only way to determine this is to keep accurate records, like other businesses do, of the number of calls and the dollars generated from these calls. That includes walk-in business resulting from your ad, as well.

B. I know there are businesses in your classification that are getting results. If you're really not getting your share of the calls, let's take a close look at what you and your competition are saying and in what size ad you're saying it.

20. YOU'RE NOT THE PHONE COMPANY.

That's correct. And because I'm not the phone company, I'm in a position to place your directory advertising in a marketed area more suited to your business needs and at a considerably lower cost.

Most telephone company boundary lines for their yellow pages directories were configured 30 or 40 years ago. The populations, communities and shopping patterns of consumers have changed greatly over the years making these boundary lines dated. Independent yellow pages directories allow you to target your market according to current shopping patterns of people in your desired area.

21. I DIDN'T GET THAT BOOK DELIVERED TO MY HOUSE.

A. I'm sorry if you didn't receive our directory when we delivered it. Actually, yellow pages directories look very similar to one another and are quite frankly taken for granted. People don't get on the phone with their neighbors to discuss who's advertising or not advertising this year. What we've discovered, when investigating situations like yours, is that the directory actually was delivered and has been stored where it's not visible.

Honestly, whether you received the directory or not shouldn't be the basis of your decision to advertise with us. That decision should be made on whether advertising in it will be profitable.

I'm being very frank with you when I say that not everyone uses the yellow pages or, for that matter, uses our directory. However, the percentage of yellow pages users who shop from our directory is large enough that businesses of all types have found it profitable to advertise with us year after year.

B. I want to assure you that distribution of our directories is taken very seriously. Our company knows it not only has an obligation to its advertisers to get their messages out to the community, but an obligation to provide people, like you, with a complete directory they can use to locate goods and services.

I'm sorry if we missed your house. While it's the intention of all yellow pages publishers to achieve 100% delivery, no one has ever done so. Realistically, you can expect distribution figures to be around 97%.

Distribution is something you should pay attention to. However, more important is whether you can make a profit by advertising in our directory. I have letters from some of our advertisers I'd like to share with you which tell how their businesses were affected by advertising with us last year.

22. I DON'T THINK PEOPLE USE YOUR BOOK.

A. What makes you say that? There are some people who know that all yellow pages are not published by the same company and choose a directory to use based on differences in circulation and features. Most of these people are business people like you who are called on by different yellow pages salespeople in the area. Yet the general population, your customer, refers to the yellow pages like they refer to a dictionary: *it's a book of information.* People don't scrutinize the binding of a dictionary to see if it's published by Funk & Wagnalls or by Webster. And they don't investigate to see who published the yellow pages directory they're about to open. People turn to the yellow pages when they need information. If the information is there, they're satisfied.

B. Are you saying that because you don't use this directory? Your real concern should be whether your customers or potential customers use it? The answer is, they do. I know that because I call on a lot of the advertisers in our book and many of them have put us through stiff testing to determine whether their ads paid off. These advertisers couldn't get positive results and wouldn't renew their ads if people weren't using our book.

23. PEOPLE THROW AWAY YOUR BOOK.

A. You're giving our salespeople an awful lot of credit and not much credit to your fellow business owners. If everyone is throwing our directory away, then the ads certainly can't be bringing in any business to our advertisers. That would mean we have one incredible sales force to be able to renew totally ineffective advertising year in and year out.

I'm sure you've advertised in various

media over the years. When you did, you must have been pretty certain whether the advertising was worth it. Your fellow business owners, our advertisers, are no different than you. They recognize when their advertising dollars are well spent, which is evident by the number of businesses that renew with us each year.

B. You may know some people who do not keep our book, and it may even be your own experience. Yet there are literally thousands of people you have no contact with who not only keep our directory, but use it extensively. I know this to be true because in doing my job, I find out the results of current advertisers. Most business owners watch their advertising dollars very carefully. After all, renewing an ineffective ad every year is very costly to a business. I'm often given extensive documentation regarding the effectiveness of their ads. Regardless of the number of people who throw away our directory or who simply don't use it, there evidently is enough usage to make it profitable for you to advertise.

24. I'VE TALKED TO MY FRIENDS AND NEIGHBORS, AND THEY DON'T USE YOUR BOOK. I'M NOT RENEWING MY AD.

A. I won't refute that your friends and neighbors don't use our directory. I'll even go you one further and admit they aren't the only ones. There are people out there who only use our competitors' directory and there are those who don't use yellow pages at all. Keep in mind though, your neighbors and friends may total 50 or 100 people. Our directory, however, is delivered to tens of thousands of people.

Many businesses who advertised with us last year were also concerned about their results. They not only wanted to know whether they had made the right decision for that year, but for the years to come as well. These businesses used a variety of methods to monitor the effectiveness of their ads. Let me show you how they did this and what they found. (Show testimonials.)

B. Remember, profitability is the most important consideration for a business in deciding whether to advertise. Even though the people you're close to say they didn't use our book, they only account for a small percentage of the people who receive the directory. We encourage all our customers to source their calls so they can be sure they've invested their money wisely. I can show you that the businesses who closely monitored their results over the entire year either renewed or increased their advertising. Wouldn't you rather make your advertising decision on the basis of facts than on guesswork? Let me demonstrate a number of ways to monitor the results of your ad this year so you'll know for certain how well the book is working for you.

25. HOW DO I KNOW YOU'LL DELIVER YOUR BOOKS?

A. It's in our best interest to deliver our books. The only reason business owners choose to advertise with us is because they feel they will make money. The only way we have of ensuring those owners of making money is to deliver their advertising message to every home and business within the directory's boundaries.

B. If our books weren't delivered, it would be impossible for our advertisers to get business from their ads, correct? Part of my job is calling on business owners like yourself, who have never advertised with us before. My other responsibilities, however, include renewing current accounts. Talking to our advertisers is one of the more satisfying parts of my job because they provide the facts as to how well their ad worked and how much the book is being used. Initially, some of them, like you, were skeptical. But, since you're not the first business to advertise with us, you have the good fortune to be able to see the results of other advertisers here in your area. (Show testimonials.)

26. PEOPLE ONLY USE THE BOOK WITH THE WHITE PAGES.

A. People only refer to the yellow pages when they need it. No one really picks up a directory for casual reading or browsing. So when that moment comes when they need something, they look in the classified section and are not particularly concerned about the alphabetical listings.

B. The yellow pages and the white pages offer two completely different kinds of information. The yellow pages provide information to people who are ready to buy but often don't know who to buy from. The white pages are referred to when someone already has a specific name in mind but needs the address or phone number. When you're needing a classification of businesses, any yellow pages directory can satisfy your needs, whether there are white pages listings attached or not.

C. Did you know there are many communities all over the country where for years the phone company has separated the yellow and white pages directories. Many newcomers to your area are used to seeing those separate yellow and white pages books. They're a prime user of yellow pages because they're unfamiliar with their new environment. You can attract their business by being in a directory format they're already familiar with.

27. JUST LEAVE IT LIKE IT IS.

A. Obviously your ad worked. You wouldn't keep it if it didn't, right? Let me ask you this: Does the heading you advertised at cover everything you sell and do? If it doesn't, you're cheating yourself out of a lot of money.

If the yellow pages gets you customers from one heading, it will get you customers from another heading. Even if that second heading represents only 10% of your business, that's still additional income to you.

B. Mr. Phillips, I know business owners have a lot of daily responsibilities like dealing with customers, taking inventory, receiving deliveries and so on. Sometimes yellow pages advertising gets associated with things like renewing ones insurance policy, a simple and quick procedure. Yet, putting your business message in front of the public for an annual publication can have a great impact on your company. Remember, advertising agencies get paid tremendous sums of money for planning and creating what to say for their clients. That effort does make a difference.

Your business, as well as your market, can change during the course of a year. More important, the competition in your classification will change each year. Yellow pages advertising requires planning, thought, and strategy to allow you to be as profitable as possible.

I've spent some time researching your account and have questions regarding your business. Maybe in the end your program will remain the same. In any case, it will certainly be beneficial to your business if we take a little time to look at your ad and what your competition has been doing.

28. I'VE GONE OVER THIS BEFORE AND I'M JUST NOT INTERESTED.

A. That's fine. Since you're entitled to a free listing in the directory, I'll just take a minute to make sure your listing information is correct.

I don't know how long you've been here, but I would imagine that since you started your business, it has gone through quite a few changes. How people shop has also changed. Today people can pick up the phone, rattle off a 16 digit credit card number, and purchase almost any type of goods or services.

People today are very conscious of time, whether they are consumers or in business, like you. Look at the explosion of the fast food industry, copy machines, FAX machines, express check-ins, express lanes and express mail.

This is especially true for the newcomer to an area, the emergency buyer, the dissatisfied customer, the individual who makes an infrequent type of purchase, and the comparison shopper. Have I mentioned any of your customers?

If yes, then you should make yourself available to them by advertising in the directory. If no, then by advertising in the yellow pages you could get these kinds of buyers as your regular customers.

B. Do you know what I do besides sell yellow pages advertising? I bring in new customers to businesses like yours. When people you've never seen before start doing business with you, you make money. You make money because you've provided a service to them. I make money because I've provided a service to you. It's a win-win situation for all three of us—you, me, and your customer. Let me show you how I've done this. (Show testimonials.)

29. ALL MY BUSINESS COMES BY WORD-OF-MOUTH.

A. Word-of-mouth business is wonderful in the sense that it means you've done a good job in providing service or products to your customers. Of course, it involves no cash outlay because your customers spread the word for you.

Consider this, Mr. Phillips. There are a lot of people who have done business with you over the years and might not remember your name and location. Or, they may have moved away or even died. It's now impossible for them to recommend you to others. Even more important, however, is this: People who need your products or services now (meaning any hour of the day) may find it too time consuming to track down friends, relatives or acquaintances to get a recommendation.

These ready buyers are unfamiliar with you. They turn to the yellow pages every day to make purchases because there is always a directory nearby, it costs them nothing to obtain, and it saves them time.

B. It wouldn't hurt your business if you discovered new ways of bringing in customers, would it? You can always have word-of-mouth business, why rely on it completely when there are *many* profitable ways of increasing your customer base. As the numbers of your customers grow, so does your word-of-mouth business. Yellow pages advertising is a proven way of attracting buyers who don't look for word-of-mouth recommendations to make their purchases.

30. I'VE DECIDED TO CANCEL ALL MY ADVERTISING.

A. I can take care of that for you since I'm responsible for your account this year. You know, our company hates to lose good advertisers like you. How come you've decided to discontinue your advertising?

B. It sounds as though you feel your ad didn't work. Let me ask you this: How have you determined your results weren't satisfactory?

C. Is it your wish to cancel because the ad didn't work? If your phone wasn't working, you wouldn't remove it, would you? You'd have it fixed! Well, think of me as your yellow pages repairman. I have a great deal of experience in determining proper text and classification, art work and ad placement to gain maximum results for my customers.

31. I'LL JUST WAIT UNTIL NEXT YEAR.

A. If I were here to deliver the money you had won from a lottery or sweepstakes, would you ask me to come back next year? I'm not implying you'll soon be able to retire by taking an ad out in this directory, but I am saying that businesses just like yours have found it very profitable advertising year after year. I haven't yet met a person in business who would rather make money tomorrow than today.

B. I realize that's another way of saying you're not interested. I visit a lot of businesses through the year and it appears to me that you have a good business going here. I'll bet that in the course of building your business into what it is today, you carefully evaluated the different opportunities that presented themselves. Why not take a look and see if some of your business problems can't be solved by yellow pages advertising? I mean, problems like getting new customers or offsetting the increasing costs of fixed expenses like rent, insurance, and utilities.

32. LET ME THINK IT OVER.

A. If you're going to think it over and have me return, you're seriously considering advertising in the directory. We covered a lot of information today. Which part of the material that we discussed did you want to think over?

B. I appreciate the time you took for us to discuss yellow pages advertising for your business. In all candor, I can't help sensing that in the way you said, "Let me think it over," you're not going to go home tonight, sit in your most comfortable chair and ponder what we've just discussed. And I doubt you'll stay up all night to give it a lot of deep thought, am I right? Probably you won't give it any thought until I call you on the phone or walk back into your store. Your decision will then be made in a matter of seconds.

I'd like you to be as straight forward with me as I'm being with you. What haven't I done to convince you that you will make money by advertising in this directory?

C. I understand that you may not be ready to finalize your advertising. As a help to me, could you let me know what it is that makes you undecided?

33. I DON'T NEED A LARGER AD.

A. The first thing I do when I'm assigned an account is to research it. That means I study the ads for copy factors, art work and overall visual effectiveness. Then I look at the classification and see what the competitors are doing. I then pretend I'm a potential customer and see which ad influences me.

Reviewing someone's yellow pages program is not like rolling over their insurance policy for the next year. It involves research and then planning a strategy that will provide the customer with an advantage over his competition. That is why I've prepared this larger ad for you. I feel it will give you the edge you need over your competition. In the long run, it will be more profitable.

B. Would you feel that way if you knew this larger ad would be more profitable than the one you're currently running? I understand there's no way of absolutely knowing that now, yet there was also no way of knowing your present ad would be profitable when you first placed it. Part of my responsibility to you, is to provide you with the most cost-effective yellow pages program for your business. I've spent some time researching your account and classifications and feel this larger ad will attract more business. Let me show you why.

34. I ONLY WANT A BOLD LISTING.

A. My experience in advertising has always been that business owners want to get the most amount of advertising for as little as possible. This, of course, is understandable. However, when determining the cost of an ad, you need to look at the dollars returned, not just the rate of the ad. The bold listing is actually the most expensive item of advertising in any yellow pages directory because it brings in the least amount of business.

I worked out a program that won't cost you money. Instead, it will make you money. Let me show you how.

B. The purpose of advertising is to attract buyers. When buyers turn to the yellow pages, in a sense, they have their money in hand. The only thing standing in the way of their spending that money is information. That's why they're referring to the yellow pages— for information. Is a company reliable? Does it have a large selection? And so on. A name, address, and phone number in bold type doesn't provide potential buyers with the information they're seeking.

C. If you and I met at a party and I asked you about your business, you wouldn't simply tell me its name, address and phone number, would you? Of course not. You'd tell me about the products and services you provide and why I should do business with you rather than with your competitors. You need to say those kinds of things in the yellow pages because that's what people looking there want to know.

35. I'M NOT INTERESTED.

A. That's fine. I'll just need a minute to make sure your name, address, and phone number are correct and that you're listed under the proper heading. (Verify information.) I've worked with many business owners who carry the exact products and provide the same services as you do. They've been very pleased over the years with the amount of new customers they've attracted through the yellow pages.

There's a large pool of buyers out there for you to tap into. All you need to do is to be competitive in your classification, and you'll get your fair share of that business.

B. I've been in sales long enough to appreciate what it's like for business owners like you. It's not easy running a business today with responsibilities like checking inventory, overseeing employees, making payroll, servicing customers and meeting a barrage of salespeople. Because business owners are called on by so many salespeople everyday, they sometimes make automatic responses rather than well thought out decisions about what they have to gain from a salesperson's visit.

My purpose in being here is to introduce you to a proven method for increasing sales. All I ask is that you make a decision, not an automatic response, based on the information I'll give you.

C. That's fine. Let me ask you one question, though. If a customer walked in here and asked if he could buy something you have in stock, would you reply "Not interested?" Of course you wouldn't. The yellow pages is no different than your store. Customers are walking through the directory asking the same question, "Where can I buy what you have in stock?"

36. CALL ME WHEN THE BOOK IS CLOSING.

A. By asking me to come back at a later date, I imagine you're seriously thinking of representing yourself in the directory. If you do decide on placing an ad, I know you'll want it to look good and to be effective. You'll also want me to provide you with professional service. There's nothing wrong in asking for those things, yet my being able to deliver them to you at the close of a directory is another matter. It would be like my suggesting I come into your store to make purchases the day after Christmas and expecting your personal attention. It's better for you, your business and our working relationship that we at least discuss your advertising needs now or within the next two weeks.

B. If it's absolutely impossible for you to finalize your advertising until the close of the directory, I'll work with you the best way I can under those circumstances. However, I hope I can appeal to you, as someone who also conducts business, to begin much sooner. You wouldn't be able to accommodate all your customers on the last day of the year, would you?

C. What I'm really hearing is that you don't think yellow pages advertising is that important to your business. If you were certain the yellow pages would bring in a lot of new customers, you wouldn't put off finalizing it until the close of the directory, would you?

Regardless if your decision is to advertise or not, wouldn't it be in the best interests of your business to arrive at a decision before the close of the book? If you want to go forward with the advertising, I can give you all the time needed for proper art work, ad copy, and show proofs to make certain everything is correct. On the other hand, if you choose not to advertise, at least that decision is behind you. You can now turn your attention to other aspects of your business.

37. THERE ARE JUST TOO MANY DIRECTORIES.

A. There were probably a lot of places in town to get a hamburger before Ray Kroc opened his first McDonalds. Yet, he turned a nice profit.

You're right, there are a lot of directories being published today, but that doesn't mean you can't profit by advertising in them.

B. The mere fact that there are a lot of directories out there and a lot of advertisers between the covers should signify that many business owners have found it profitable to be there. Did you know that of all the advertising media available today, the yellow pages has experienced, by far, the greatest growth? Growth in our industry means there's been a good return on dollars invested by businesses like yours.

C. There are a lot of directories out there because both consumers and business owners have various directory needs. Some businesses only draw from a small area while others can attract and service customers from many communities. Some consumers prefer to shop close to home while others are willing to travel great distances to satisfy their needs. Fortunately for you, you now have a choice in placing your advertising in a directory that best suits your business.

38. I USE OTHER FORMS OF ADVERTISING.

A. Most other advertising media, such as newspapers, magazines, radio and T.V., are known as creative advertising. This simply means that they create a desire in a consumer to buy. As you know, these forms of advertising can be profitable for businesses. What often happens with creative advertising, however, is this: 1) Someone hears or sees your ad but is not ready to buy. By the time he is, he can't recall your location or name, and 2) Someone hears or sees your ad and is ready to buy. But because he's unable to write down your name or location (he's driving by a billboard or listening to the radio) your advertising efforts are wasted.

Yellow pages advertising is directive advertising. It directs a buyer to a seller. This form of advertising actually complements all forms of creative advertising by acting as a memory jogger to a perspective customer.

You'll also discover that yellow pages advertising can stand on its own. Many people who are ready to buy, but don't know who to buy from, turn to the yellow pages.

B. It sounds as though you've found certain advertising media to work for you, and that's great. What I'd like to do is to show you how another advertising format can also be profitable for your business.

Nearly all advertising media, such as newspapers, T.V. and radio, are referred to as creative advertising—they create a desire in an individual to buy. Yellow pages is different. They direct a consumer where to buy a product or service, that's why it's called directive advertising.

Let's talk about sales for a minute.

You and I are both salespeople, and we're familiar with the terms "easy sale" and "tough sale."

With creational advertising, your objective is to sell someone something they hadn't given much thought to before being exposed to your advertising message. You also need to convince them to purchase the product or service through you, not someone else. With yellow pages advertising, buyers have already decided they want to buy a particular product. Your only task is to get them to do business with *you*, not your competitor.

Wouldn't you agree it's much easier to sell someone in need of your product or service rather than someone who is not?

C. That's even more reason to advertise in the yellow pages. Pretend you are a consumer being exposed to an advertised message. You're not in a position to make a purchase that instant. A day, a week, or even a month goes by before you're ready to buy.

Which advertising media would be most readily available?

What will appeal to you about the yellow pages is that it's so inexpensive to keep your advertising message in front of so many people for such a long period of time. It's working for you 24 hours a day, 365 days a year compared to the short life span of creational media (2 hours for a newspaper or 15-30 seconds for T.V. or radio).

Don't you think it makes good business sense to have your advertising message in front of people who are ready to buy your particular product or service?

39. EVERYBODY KNOWS ME.

A. Everybody may know you, but does everybody do business with you? I think you'll agree that most of the products and services you offer can also be found at other businesses. This means they have their customers, too, or they wouldn't be open for business.

A great many people purchase items, like the ones you carry, through the yellow pages. You're entitled to this business as much as anyone else. Let me show you how you can capitalize on yellow pages advertising.

B. Aren't you really saying that the people you do business with know you? Your customer base is always changing. There are a great many people in this area that were too young to do business with you right up until this year. Now they've reached an age or found themselves in a position to need the products you carry. Since they've never made these kinds of purchases before, it's likely they don't know you have them or, for that matter, anyone who has them. That's why they'll turn to their yellow pages.

C. Probably when you started your business, people didn't move as much as they do today. They tended to continue to live where they were born and raised. But it's a different story today. America is a very mobile and transient society. In many areas, 20% of the population has an address change every year.

When people move in to your market area for the first time, it's impossible for them to be familiar with you and the services you provide. Newcomers rely heavily on yellow pages for that very reason. They simply aren't familiar with their new environment.

D. Usually when someone says "everybody knows me," it's because they've been in business for a long time. Let me ask you, hasn't your business changed over the years? Aren't you carrying new and different products from those you started with?

I'm sure there are a number of people who don't make a connection between you and the products you've added over the years. They may have you in mind for one or more things but rely on your competitors for others.

You need to keep everybody up to date on what you have to offer.

E. Don't you sometimes lose customers? Let me show you how you may have lost some and how you can turn that to your advantage.

If you look at your classification here in the directory, you'll notice all your competitors advertising what they carry and offer. Some of your customers turn to these pages looking for you, but are seduced by other ads that supply so much more information.

You could keep these customers by properly representing yourself in the directory. You might also capture some of your competitor's customers as well.

40. MY COMPETITION HAS ONLY A LISTING.

A. Shouldn't your decision to advertise in the yellow pages be based on whether your business will benefit rather than on who else is advertising in the classification?

I'm sure if we listed everything about your company right down to your credit policy or where you currently advertise and made the same type of list for your competitor, there would be many differences.

You can take advantage of the fact that your competitor is not capitalizing on the types of buyers who use the yellow pages everyday. I'm referring to newcomers in your area, emergency buyers, dissatisfied customers from competing businesses, infrequent buyers and comparison shoppers.

These first-time buyers can become lifelong customers and even provide countless recommendations to others in your area.

B. Are you familiar with the saying or slogan, "developing an edge?" It couldn't have more meaning or importance than in business. Since your competition only has a listing, you could capture all the business of people who refer to the directory when they're ready to buy, but don't have anyone in mind to buy from.

41. I HAVE MORE BUSINESS THAN I CAN HANDLE.

A. Many companies I call on are in the same position. However, the owners of these companies have decided to continue their representation in the yellow pages to attract more desirable and profitable buyers.

B. It's one thing to be busy and another to have exactly the types of customers you want. Through yellow pages advertising you can position your business in a way to draw in the types of customers you prefer and the most profitable jobs.

C. If you've been in business a while, you know that business conditions are anything but stagnant. Things could be steady or growing for a long time and then suddenly drop off.

There's something called a customer cycle which every business faces. Some of the people you're doing business with today will move away, no longer need your services, pass away, have poor credit, or for one reason or another, not be fully satisfied. About 10% of a business' customer base falls into this category each year. You will need to replace these customers with new customers. The yellow pages has helped businesses like yours do just that.

42. YELLOW PAGES ISN'T FOR MY KIND OF BUSINESS.

A. Have you ever advertised before in the yellow pages? Without ever having advertised before, why do you feel your business wouldn't profit like the many others in your line who do?

B. Do you know what types of buyers use the yellow pages? They are newcomers to the area, emergency buyers, buyers who are dissatisfied with your competitors, buyers who are making an infrequent purchase and buyers who are comparing prices. These categories represent a tremendous number of people you could be doing business with if only you made yourself visible to them.

43. MY AD DOESN'T PULL LIKE IT USED TO.

A. First, let's be certain that that's the case. If so, we can take a close look at the various factors that could account for that. How have you been sourcing your calls to determine your ad's effectiveness?

There are several factors that could contribute to your ad pulling in less business: 1) There could be more advertisers at your classification which means you have a smaller share of the market, 2) Some of your competitors could have a more effective ad, 3) The copy factors in your ad may not be as complete as they could be, 4) There are now more competing directories in the area, and 5) Your phone may not be answered as effectively as in the past.

We have a great deal of control over many of these factors. The important thing to keep in mind about any advertising is whether it pays for itself. Even though your ad doesn't pull like it used to, it still can be profitable for your business and is a cost-effective way of bringing in new customers every month.

B. Let's take a look at your ad and the classification to see if we can determine what may be causing that. If there's something wrong with your ad we can fix it. Of course, your ad could be an effective one. What we find is that ads don't pull in the same amount of business every year for a number of reasons. For example, you may have more competitors than before, conditions in your industry could be slow, or the state of the economy may be at fault. These conditions are always changing which means your ad could very well bring in more business this year than last year.

44. LET ME TALK TO MY PARTNER.

A. I've worked with a great many businesses where more than one person made the advertising decisions. It's always proved best to have all decision makers and the yellow pages representative sit down together to discuss the advertising. That way everyone's time is managed better. All the information regarding your business and my company is available, and everyone's viewpoint is represented. When is the best time for all of us to meet?

B. How do you feel about what we've discussed today? Well, then, if I can get together with you and your partner, we can set up a yellow pages program that will benefit your business and be acceptable to both of you. When would be the best time for us to do that?

45. I DO NO LOCAL BUSINESS.

A. With advancements in telecommunications, travel and media, people conduct their business differently from the way they did many years ago.

Purchasing agents, for instance, request yellow pages directories from around the country to find new sources of suppliers. Local directories are also used by out of town business people at airports, hotels, motels, libraries, and chambers of commerce.

You can capture this business from people who are ready to buy, but who do not know who to buy from.

B. Let me ask you something. If a company in this local area wanted to place an order for your product or service, would you do business with them? Of course you would.

There are always companies looking for new suppliers because of things like service, price or availability. With no representation in the yellow pages, it's impossible for you to capture these buyers. You'll never be able to measure the number of orders you didn't get.

46. MY BUSINESS IS SEASONAL.

I know I don't have to tell you that with a seasonal business, it is vital to maximize business during peak times. Yellow pages advertising is an excellent way of ensuring that your business remains strong during your busy times and even provides business during your slow periods.

The yellow pages can accomplish this because your ad is placed in every single home and business within your targeted market area 24 hours a day, 365 days a year.

It's important to understand that even if you bring in no business during your off season, you need to measure the effectiveness of your advertising over the entire year. As long as your return exceeds your cost, it is profitable for you.

47. WE HAVE OUR OWN SALES FORCE.

A. Being a salesperson myself and being part of a sales force, let me share with you how I approach my job. I work on commission, so I have plenty of incentive to put in a very full day to cover my monthly overhead and to meet my personal goal of saving for future investments.

On my very best day, I can realistically

expect to write business with no more than 5 customers. I would imagine there are far more than 5 customers (or 5 times your entire sales force) who are ready to do business with you every day.

Not only that, but I'm off on weekends, I take a 2-week vacation every year, and I'm occasionally ill or off the job for an emergency. Your ad in the yellow pages, however, carries to the ready buyer 24 hours a day, all year long.

B. Great! What I'd like to do is have you interview my client for a position on your sales force. Here's his background.

You won't have to cover him with any medical or dental insurance. He won't take any paid or even unpaid vacations. He's never been ill. He works weekends and holidays. As a matter of fact, he's never off the market. He has the ability to clone himself into thousands and be exactly where your customers are when they're ready to buy. Let me introduce you to your next star salesperson, the yellow pages.

C. Did you know this directory is a salesperson too? The difference though between your salespeople and my salesperson is that your salespeople call on a number of prospects trying to create a desire in them to buy. My salesperson gets called on by your prospects when they're ready to buy.

48. CAN YOU GUARANTEE THE POSITION I WANT?

A. No yellow pages salespeople, regardless of the company they represent, can guarantee a particular position in a directory.

While larger ads get a better position and will generate more calls than smaller ads, a properly designed program including smaller ads can still be profitable for your business.

If you are interested in the maximum

amount of calls through yellow pages advertising, I've been trained to accomplish that for you.

B. The answer to your question is no. No one knows where any ad will appear until the directory closes and is completely paged. But that shouldn't deter you from advertising in the yellow pages. You may have a particular position for your ad in mind based on where *your* eyes tend to go when looking in a directory. But there are many factors besides position that affect the amount of business your ad will bring in. Let me show you what I mean.

C. No, I'm sorry I cannot. I assume it's the position at the front of the classification that you'd like.

Yes, studies have shown that ads at the beginning of the classification receive more calls. But businesses that place ads that fall in the middle or rear of a classification find they, too, can be profitable.

When you notice a heavily advertised

classification, it tells you a lot of businesses have found it worthwhile to be there. The smaller ads at the back of the classification are renewed each year, as well. This is another strong indication that you can still make money regardless of where your ad is placed.

49. MY BUSINESS IS TOO SMALL.

A. You may not be aware of this, but the yellow pages is designed especially for small businesses. There really is no other advertising medium where you can place your business card with a message in every home and business in your market place for pennies a day. Not only that, but you're able to compete with the largest of your competitors since there is a limit to the number of ads a business can place at each heading.

You may know you're small but there's no way for the consumers to know that when they're looking at your ad.

B. Did you know that the yellow pages are often referred to as the small business advertising bible? Depending upon how much you wish to invest, there is a wide range of ads to choose from. When yellow pages users turn to your classification, it's as if they were on a street of similar businesses. You have as good a chance as anyone of having that consumer choose your business. All you need is an effective sign telling them why they should come inside.

50. I'M SELLING MY BUSINESS.

A. When you sell something— a house, a car, or in your case, a business— you want to make it as attractive as possible to a potential buyer. An existing yellow pages program can be a strong selling point. It shows a potential buyer of your business that its message is already in every home and business in the area. Until your business sells, which could take longer than you expect, you'll be benefiting from the revenues brought in by your ads.

B. Having a good program in the yellow pages can actually be an asset when selling your business. To a prospective buyer, a business that is currently advertising is apt to be a healthier business than one that doesn't do any advertising. Therefore, your business can command a better price.

51. THERE ARE ALREADY TOO MANY ADS AT MY HEADING.

A. That should be an indication to you that it's a profitable classification. Otherwise, advertisers at that heading wouldn't renew their ads year after year.

B. I work this directory each year and am familiar with some of the businesses that advertise in the classification. Some of our largest advertisers under your classification didn't start out that way. They ran small display ads or even incolumn ads. Over the years they've increased the size of their ads because they got results. Even though there is a lot of competition at your heading, there is also a lot of buying activity.

C. A lot of ads at a heading are like a lot of fishermen on a lake. Chances are the fishing is pretty good when a spot is so populated. If there were few anglers out there, you could assume the fishing wasn't too good.

52. MINE IS A CASH AND CARRY BUSINESS.

A. Even though you may associate the yellow pages with the telephone, a great many people refer to the directory and then proceed to a business location. A lot of cash and carry businesses advertise in the yellow pages just so they can capitalize on the walk-in trade.

B. Remember, the yellow pages is a buyer's information guide. By placing an ad in the directory, you are not just soliciting telephone calls you're also appealing to the general public who is seeking information to assist them in buying. By mentioning the reliability of your company, the years you've been in business, the completeness of your service, your location or your low prices, you can influence the shopper to do business with you.

53. I'VE HAD A LOT OF PROBLEMS WITH YOUR COMPANY.

A. Probably the biggest responsibility I have to my company is generating sales, but the biggest responsibility I have to my customers is providing good service. Why don't you share with me the problems you're talking about. Maybe I can be of some help to you.

B. You shouldn't be afraid to put your sales representative to work. When you have a problem with our company, it's my responsibility to solve the problem as quickly as possible. We profit by having you as a paid advertiser, and you profit by representing yourself in our directory. That's known as a win-win situation, and nothing should get in its way.

54. I'M MOVING.

A. That makes it even more important for you to advertise in the directory. You've probably worked very hard to get the customers you already have, and you certainly want to retain their business. What better way of letting them know you're still in business but at a new location than by placing that information in each of their homes? Of course, you'll also be attracting new customers by advertising that you're new to the area and where you can be found.

B. If you're still going to be doing business in this area but don't know where you'll be moving to, let me show you how we can keep buyers in touch with you.

Of course, if you have your new location before we go to print, we'll make sure it gets in the directory. However, if it's too late to include your new address, it still is beneficial for your business to advertise.

A good deal of directory business comes through the telephone. You'll be able to capitalize on telephone inquiries by providing the caller with your new address. Don't forget your old customers, either. They may pass by your former location and think you've gone out of business. They'll be turning to the yellow pages, looking for someone to replace you. Your ad will let them know you're still doing business as usual, but at a new location.

55. I NEVER ADVERTISE.

A. There are businesses, like yours, who never advertise and are profitable. As a business owner who obviously is focused on profit, why not realize the profits that yellow pages advertising can generate for you? Why not experience how yellow pages can be a catalyst for making your business grow even more?

By your own admission, you've never tried it, so you can't be passing judgment based on experience. Others in the same business as you, however, remain visible in the yellow pages year after year. This is a strong indication that it pays off.

B. You are very fortunate that conditions in your marketplace allow you to have a successful business without advertising. Those conditions, though, could change— and change abruptly. What if one or more competitors were to open in your area and aggressively go after your business by advertising in the yellow pages? Who would new-comers to the area— big yellow pages users— be likely to do business with?

56. I'D ONLY GET NUISANCE CALLS.

A. Even without any advertising, you will still receive your share of nuisance calls. Why not offset some of those nuisance calls with profit-producing calls?

When an ad brings you a customer you wouldn't have otherwise gotten, it not only creates an immediate profitable transaction for you, but it also builds your referral business. And your word-of-mouth business can increase geometrically with each new customer.

B. By the way you phrased your objection, it sounds as though you've never tried yellow pages advertising. I won't tell you that you'll never receive a nuisance call from the yellow pages, but you'll find the profitable calls outweigh the unprofitable ones. Besides, your ad can be designed to eliminate most nuisance calls.

People don't pick up a yellow pages directory to browse through it or for light reading. They use the directory as an information guide when they're ready to make a purchase. How many nuisance calls are you likely to get from a market made up of people ready to buy your product or service?

C. Consumers use the yellow pages because it provides them with pertinent buying information they need when they're about to make a purchase. Very often they refer to a directory and go directly to the business. By not being properly represented in the yellow pages, you're trading all those paying customers through your front door for a few less trips to your telephone.

Remember, even if you do receive nuisance calls (and all businesses do), if you treat them well they may become a very profitable customer in the months or years to follow.

57. MY LOCATION BRINGS IN ALL MY BUSINESS.

A. It's no wonder since you're doing no advertising. You've been relying solely on your location to get your cash register to ring. There are other ways, though, of capitalizing on your excellent location. One in particular has been proven effective for more than 100 years. I'm speaking, of course, of yellow pages advertising. Let me show you how that works.

B. The market from which you attract

customers is the number of people who pass by your location. Yet, not everyone who passes by your store is interested in doing business with you.

There's another market from which you can draw business which is far greater in numbers. Since you believe in location so strongly, build yourself a second one for the people who don't pass by your store— in the yellow pages.

C. I'm sure you pay a premium in rent to attract your customers. Yellow pages advertising is another way of attracting customers, but it's different in two respects: 1) It's extremely cost effective because it's inexpensive and reaches such a large number of people, and 2) People who refer to a directory are buying, not browsing or passing by.

58. I HAVE NO COMPETITION.

A. One doesn't have to go back many years to remember when you couldn't get 24 hour delivery of documents and packages. Federal Express pioneered that service, and at one time they could have made the same claim you've just made. Today, there is a long list of companies providing that same service, including the U.S. Post Office.

Our free enterprise system encourages people to copy what works. To secure the business you have today and to prevent competitors from entering your market and stealing your customers, you need to advertise.

B. You're really in a very enviable situation as there are few businesses that have no competitors. However, you still need to be concerned about the public knowing what you have to sell. The most cost-effective way of getting that type of information to the greatest number of people is through the yellow pages.

59. I CAN'T GET GOOD HELP.

I know that can be a problem for some businesses today. But getting good help is really a separate issue from advertising in the yellow pages.

You may be thinking, "What am I going to do with more business when I don't have the help to service it?"

The answer is you can be more selective about the type of work you do. You can service the jobs that are the most profitable or that you simply prefer.

60. WILL YOU GUARANTEE IT WORKS?

Have you ever gotten a guarantee from any other type of advertising? Well, yellow pages is no different. But let's take a look at the risk because that's what you're really concerned about, isn't it?

Yellow pages is not a new concept. For over a hundred years it's provided free information to ready buyers. If you were to travel anywhere today in the United States (or in many foreign countries) you would find businesses like yours represented in the yellow pages year after year. Isn't that a good indication to you that yellow pages advertising works?

61. PEOPLE DON'T LOOK AT BIG ADS.

A. What makes you say that? Perhaps a friend of yours told you he doesn't look at big ads or maybe you don't. In order to say that about all yellow pages users, you would need a great deal more data.

Actually, the entire yellow pages format is based on just the opposite idea. People do look at the larger ads and often refer to them first. Extensive research by companies both inside and outside the yellow pages industry proves this. Let me show you a couple of these surveys.

B. When people refer to the yellow pages it's because they need buying information. Why would they make their task more difficult by having to search for that information, and, once discovering it, having it be limited?

C. Actually, research has shown the opposite to be true. When you stop to think about it, it makes sense. Larger ads are easier to read and contain eye-catching art work. The concept of drawing a reader's eye by using illustrations is not unique to the yellow pages. You can see it in all types of printed advertising, such as billboards and newspapers.

62. AS A PROFESSIONAL, I HAVE AN ETHICAL PROBLEM ABOUT ADVERTISING IN THE YELLOW PAGES.

A. Why is it you feel that way? Even though your business is different from a retail or service business, it's still a business. You went to school, studied and trained for years so you could make a living in your field. You need patients or clients the same as an electrician needs customers.

Advertising in the yellow pages is really a low key approach to attaining new customers. You're not trying to create a desire in these people to do business with you. Rather, you're directing them to you when they've already decided they are in need of your particular service.

B. There's usually a greater sense of need or urgency when the services of a professional are needed as compared to retail businesses. People who turn to the yellow pages are in need of a product or service. Whether it's a professional obligation, like a Hippocratic oath, or a sense of personal pride, shouldn't you make yourself visible to these people who are seeking your help?

63. THE BIG BOYS IN MY LINE DON'T ADVERTISE IN THE YELLOW PAGES.

A. That doesn't mean *you* couldn't profit by advertising in the yellow pages. The yellow pages were originally designed for small businesses like yours. Today, even though there are many large national companies advertising, the yellow pages primarily consists of ads from Mom and Pop businesses.

B. That's really fortunate because you can take advantage of that by capturing the business of people who need your product or service but don't know who can provide it for them.

C. One reason some large companies do not advertise in the yellow pages is because they're not allowed to dominate a heading by placing large multiple display ads. However, in newspapers and on radio and television, large firms can present a powerful image and often have the capital to do just that.

So if the big boys in your line don't represent themselves, that leaves the classification wide open for you to attract new customers.

D. If you spoke to three successful insurance agents, you would probably discover that they didn't run their businesses in the exact same way.

There are many ways of making a profit. The merchandising methods of a large firm are likely to be different from yours because: 1) They have a large number of employees to generate business; 2) They have highly-skilled outside sales personnel; 3) They are located on prime real estate; or 4) They have a great deal of money allocated for media like newspaper, T.V. and radio.

A proven advertising medium for the small business is the yellow pages. You are exactly who the book was designed for.

64. YELLOW PAGES ADVERTISING WOULD LOCK ME IN FOR TOO LONG A PERIOD OF TIME.

A. I realize your business may change over the course of one year, but I'm sure you offer some things regularly that can be mentioned under the proper yellow pages heading. Whatever you sell, there are always newcomers to the area, emergency situations arising, dissatisfied customers from your competition and infrequent or comparison shoppers who refer to the yellow pages constantly.

B. The fact that the life of the directory is one year can be an advantage to you. Most advertising that's available to businesses like yours has several rate changes during the course of a year. Because there is more than one issue or spot, your advertisement is either thrown away or forgotten. Yellow pages directories are kept for an entire year, making your message available during that time to all the homes and businesses in your market area.

C. If telephone directories had shorter lives, publishers' printing costs would rise significantly and would be reflected in increased rates to you. One of the main reasons yellow pages advertising has been around for such a long time and is growing faster today than any other advertising medium is its cost effectiveness. So, it's really to your advantage that the yellow pages has a lifespan of one year.

65. I DEAL ONLY WITH A FEW FIRMS.

A. That may be true today, but business conditions can change, and change rather quickly. By dealing with only a few firms, you have a narrow customer base. If one or two of those companies stopped doing business with you for any reason, that could be devastating to your profit picture. Advertising in the yellow pages is a way of ensuring you get your share of new customers to replace any you might lose.

B. That's why I'd like to discuss a yellow pages program with you. Because you deal with fewer firms, each one is extremely important to you. So it would follow that each new customer you get has a high dollar potential. I'm sure there are other firms that could use your product or service, but unless you tell them about it, you could very well be limiting your current profits and future growth.

C. Most companies feel that their best customer is their competitor's best prospect. Since you deal with only a few firms, I'm sure each one is extremely important to you. The loss of one account would be a hardship, but gaining a new one adds security and profit. Advertising in the yellow pages can provide you with insurance against losing your current customers and the opportunity to attract new ones.

66. I'LL ONLY DEAL WITH LAST YEAR'S SALESPERSON.

A. I understand how you feel. You probably established a good working relationship with the salesperson from last year. I, myself, would like to work with the same advertisers each year for a similar reason. Unfortunately, in this industry it's just not possible. Let me explain why.

Yellow pages sales forces are comprised of large numbers of salespeople whose responsibility it is to call on a much larger number of businesses. Each business represents a certain dollar value of yellow pages advertising which changes from year to year. To be fair and equitable to its salespeople, a publisher needs to assign approximately the same dollar value of advertising to each of its sales representatives. Some yellow pages companies are bound to do this by union agreement while others simply find it's the most practical way of assigning accounts.

B. I know how you feel. Some of my customers from last year request I take care of them again this year. Unfortunately, it just isn't practical. A lot of yellow pages companies print directories in many different areas, and salespeople are often transferred when there's a shortage of help. Also, salespeople sometimes decide to go into management or are simply no longer with the company. For these reasons, it just may be impossible for last year's salesperson to work with you this year. In addition, to make things equitable, accounts are assigned randomly on an equal dollar basis. That's why you usually see a different salesperson each year.

That may not, however, be such bad news to you. I've had a great deal of training and experience in yellow pages advertising and many of my customers feel the same way about me as you feel about your salesperson from last year. It can be beneficial to your business to have another consultant's ideas as far as the copy factors in your ad, your artwork and the overall strategy for establishing the most cost-effective program for you this year.

67. I DON'T WANT TO BE ASSOCIATED WITH THE RIFF-RAFF AT MY HEADING.

A. I realize you know a great deal about these other businesses because you're all in the same line, competing in the same marketplace. On the other hand, consumers don't have this inside knowledge. As a matter of fact, that's why they're looking in the yellow pages. They're ready to buy your particular product or service, but they don't know who to buy it from. What do you think they'll be influenced by— an ad that gives them the information they're looking for, or a name, address, and telephone number?

B. People don't associate one company with another just because they're both in the yellow pages any more than they associate one company with another because they're both in the same type of business. The most important thing for any business that wants to stay open or grow is sales. Why would you want to hand over your potential customers to a competitor, particularly one who you don't think much of?

68. I HAD A BAD EXPERIENCE WITH AN INDEPENDENT DIRECTORY COMPANY.

A. If you had a bad experience with a particular model of car, you might choose not to buy it again. But surely you wouldn't go back to a horse and buggy. Having a bad experience with one company in an industry shouldn't reflect on the value of another. All I ask is that you take a look at what we offer and decide if it would benefit your business.

B. If you had a good experience with an independent directory company, would you stop me after I introduced myself and my company and say, "Where do I sign?" Certainly not. You would want to know something about our background, what we do, and how we do it before committing any of your advertising dollars. Why is that decision making process any different just because you had an unpleasant experience with a completely different company?

69. THERE AREN'T MANY ADS AT MY CLASSIFICATION.

A. That's clearly to your advantage. The greater the number of ads in a classification, the greater number of choices the consumer has, and consequently the less chance your ad has to be selected. Doesn't it make more business sense to be one advertiser among six than one among fifteen? We call it having a greater share of the market.

B. When I hear someone complain about the number of ads at a particular classification, it's usually because there are too many. "There are so many ads, why would someone select mine?" Certainly, with your classification not yet being fully developed, you stand an excellent chance of having a ready buyer decide to do business with you.

70. LET ME SEE HOW YOUR BOOK DOES THIS YEAR.

A. Can you tell me how you'll go about that task? If our book does great this year, how will you know if you're not in it? You'll want to advertise in this book if it's profitable and you won't want to advertise in it if it is not. Isn't that the bottom line? You'll never be able to determine that unless you place an ad for *your* business and monitor *your* results.

B. Does our book doing well mean whether other businesses make money by advertising in it? That really should be the

sole determining factor. You don't need to wait 'til next year for the answer. Let me show you some of the results our advertisers are getting right now in your area.
(Show testimonials.)

NOTES